the
new
bff

Being
Financially
Free

*Dear Shelley —
Here's to
Being financially —
and traveling the world
in style!
Love, Natala xo*

*Dear Shelley!
Looking forward to
traveling together!
Dream Big!
Love Diane*

the
new

Being
Financially
Free

From **Stay-at-Home Mom**
to **Stay-at-Home Mompreneur**

natalia yosco

fine free
MEDIA

Nashville, TN

the new bff :
being financially free

From **Stay-at-Home Mom**
to **Stay-at-Home Mompreneur**

Copyright © 2012 by Natalia Yosco

This book is about my journey and where it is leading me. Of course, no two journeys are the same and there can be no guarantee that any path taken will lead to success. Results achieved in network marketing may vary depending on a number of factors, including your level of effort, the area in which you live, business experience, diligence and leadership. This book shares the steps I've taken on my path to success in the hopes that a similar journey will lead to success for you.

Printed in the United States of America

10 9 8 7 6 5 4 3

ISBN-13: 978-0-9857626-3-6

fine free
MEDIA

Fine Free Media LLC
Nashville, TN

www.FineFreeMedia.com

Edited by: Graham Van Dixhorn, Write To Your Market, Inc.

Cover and Interior Design: Peri Gabriel, Knockout Design,
www.knockoutbooks.com

Cover Copy: Graham Van Dixhorn, Write To Your Market, Inc.
www.writetoyourmarket.com

contents

acknowledgements

No woman is an island. I would like to thank all women, especially those who embrace and promote entrepreneurism of all kinds. You are a big part of my inspiration and motivation to write this book, and to share my success with the world.

I want to express my deep and abiding appreciation to my business partners, my team, for their wit, wisdom, energy and enthusiasm. We've shared more than a dream, and we've realized more than our goals. Without you there is no road to BFF.

Another team has made it possible for this book to come to life: my book production team. I'm especially grateful to Graham Van Dixhorn of Write To Your Market, Inc., and to Peri Gabriel of Knockout Design for their professional guidance and support.

Lastly, I wish to thank my husband, John, and our three beautiful children, Daphne, Hunter, and Scarlett. Though I tell you every day, and hope you know how deeply it's felt, I love you all beyond words. You ARE my life, my present joy, and my future of limitless hope and happiness. Thank you from the center of my soul for the gift of being your wife and mother.

introduction

"You are responsible for your life, and when you get that everything changes. Don't wait for anyone else to fix you, to save you or complete you. No one completes you. When you get that you are responsible for your life, you get free."

OPRAH WINFREY

I want to share a brief story about a woman I know of whose life resembles so many of ours, perhaps more or less difficult than yours. She was raised in a nice home, with decent and loving parents, and she went to a small college as a young adult. She held various jobs and positions, and married a man with whom she had a child, but after only a year they separated and then divorced, and the woman's life started to fall apart. She was diagnosed with clinical depression, and even thought about suicide. She took odd work where she could get it, having very nearly given up on dreams she had once had.

About that period, she states, "I was the biggest failure I knew." Divorced, jobless and a single parent, here is what happened next:

"Failure meant a stripping away of the inessential. I stopped pretending to myself that I was anything other than what I was, and began to direct all my energy to finishing the only work that mattered to me. Had I really succeeded at anything else, I might never have found the determination to succeed in the one area where I truly belonged. I was set free, because my greatest fear had been realized, and I was still alive, and I still had a daughter whom I adored, and I had an old typewriter, and a big idea. And so rock bottom became a solid foundation on which I rebuilt my life."

Just a few short years later, this woman became one of the most famous people in the world. She has been doused with literary and philanthropic awards of all kinds, and is one of the wealthiest women in her home country. Yes, it's the story of Joanne Rowling, known to the world as J.K. Rowling, among the wealthiest and most success-ful authors of all time. The quote from above was delivered in her Harvard commencement address in 2008.

I tell you this story because I think it's easy for us to forget our dreams, and give up on the lives we were meant to live. Everyone's story is different. But we all share a need for freedom and security and happiness. We're just not always sure how to go about getting there.

Just a few short years ago, I was a stay-at-home mom, juggling my three children and worried every day about my family's financial future. My husband makes good money, but his business—in the financial services sector—isn't one that provides a steady stream of income. My kids were getting older and the cost of meeting their needs was going through the roof. And I didn't have much professional experience other than ice skating. I felt like I was in a financial vise with no foreseeable chance for release.

Today, just three short years later, I am still a stay-at-home mom, but also a business owner with success and financial security beyond any of my wildest dreams. I have business partners in every state in the nation—and even Puerto Rico! These are smart, driven people who share my desire for financial freedom. If I told you how much I make every month, you'd have to wonder if I'd tapped a new vein of gold no one knew about.

Well, I did tap a vein of gold, and, while lots of people know about it, far fewer take advantage of it. I created this book to help you decide several things.

First, are you sick and tired of being in a financial vise? Second, do you crave financial freedom badly enough to act, and to follow through? Third, do you understand and know how to take advantage of the power of residual income? And fourth, is what I have done a good fit for you?

chapter

being financially free

"A big part of financial freedom is having your heart and mind free from worry about the what-ifs of life."

SUZE ORMAN

Financial freedom. What a concept! We hear stories about it, dream about it, know people who seem to have it. But what does being financially free really mean? And how in the world do you go about achieving it?

Think back to your childhood dreams and wishes. We all had them, we all imagined what our lives would be like when we grew up. Many of us painted a fairy tale of charming princes, beautiful castles, and even brightly dressed children riding ponies and chasing butterflies. Or we saw ourselves as movie stars, champion athletes, rich and powerful women. We'd be free to come and go as we pleased, buy what we wanted, and never worry about money.

I was one of those girls who dreamed about having my dad walk me down the aisle at my wedding. Unfortunately, I lost my dad in my early teen years, and that single event changed my life forever. At that moment, I realized there are some things in life you can't control, regardless of what you do or dream. It's important to know the difference between things we can control and things we can't control. With this book, I'm here to tell you that you CAN have control of your financial well-being.

Even as grownups, most of us still dream of the future, but with some distinct differences from our childhood dreams. Now we'd be living the dream if we could pay off our debts, send our kids to college, and put enough away for a comfortable retirement! What we're really wishing for is financial freedom. It's crucial that we understand that, as women, we deserve and can create the life of our dreams. I came across this piece recently and think it says it so well:

A WOMAN SHOULD HAVE . . .

enough money within her control to move out
and rent a place of her own,
even if she never wants to or needs to . . .
something perfect to wear if the employer,
or date of her dreams wants to see her in an hour . . .

A WOMAN SHOULD HAVE . . .

a youth she's content to leave behind . . .
a past juicy enough that she's looking forward to
retelling it in her old age . . .

a set of screwdrivers, a cordless drill, and a black lace bra . . .

one friend who always makes her laugh . . .

and one who lets her cry . . .

A WOMAN SHOULD HAVE . . .

a good piece of furniture not previously owned

by anyone else in her family . . .

eight matching plates, wine glasses with stems,

and a recipe for a meal

that will make her guests feel honored . . .

A WOMAN SHOULD HAVE . . .

a feeling of control over her destiny . . .

EVERY WOMAN SHOULD KNOW . . .

how to quit a job,

break up with a lover,

and confront a friend without

ruining the friendship . . .

how to fall in love without losing herself . . .

EVERY WOMAN SHOULD KNOW . . .

when to try harder . . . and WHEN TO WALK AWAY . . .

EVERY WOMAN SHOULD KNOW . . .

that she can't change the length of her calves,

the width of her hips, or the nature of her parents . . .

that her childhood may not have been perfect . . .

but it's over . . .

EVERY WOMAN SHOULD KNOW . . .

what she would and wouldn't do for love or more . . .

how to live alone . . . even if she doesn't like it . . .

EVERY WOMAN SHOULD KNOW . . .

whom she can trust,

whom she can't,

and why she shouldn't take it personally . . .

EVERY WOMAN SHOULD KNOW . . .

where to go . . .

be it to her best friend's kitchen table . . .

or a charming Inn in the woods . . .

when her soul needs soothing . . .

EVERY WOMAN SHOULD KNOW . . .

What she can and can't accomplish in a day . . .

a month . . . and a year . . .

PAMELA REDMOND SATRAN

Glamour, May, 1997

Financial freedom means having essentially unlimited income without having to devote every minute of your life to earning it. It means you can structure your professional life around your real-life priorities. It means not having your choices limited by money. But all that can seem like a fantasy for someone who's lost it all or is struggling to make ends meet.

Working women, especially those with kids, often find themselves in a financial rut of too many expenses and a static, limited income. Choices seem limited. Dreams go unrealized. And financial worries don't just limit what's possible, they impact our lives down to the core of our being, including how we feel about ourselves and those around us.

How many of us never get to the point of feeling like we've become our fullest, best selves? How do we even know what we're capable of being when so much of our time and attention is whittled away by stress and worry or devoted to making enough money just to get by?

Even women whose spouses earn a good income face financial challenges that limit their independence and reduce opportunities for themselves and their families.

And, as it turns out, money may indeed buy happiness (or at least give us a better attitude about our lives and our futures). But you may be surprised to see how much (or how little) it takes to make a difference. According to an April, 2012 article on the website www.BusinessNewsDaily.com, a survey conducted by the Marist Institute for Public Opinion at Marist College asked people to rate their satisfaction across a number of common life conditions like family, housing, free time, and more, and then asked them about their annual household income. It turns out that an annual income of $50,000 or above made a big difference in how people ranked their happiness and personal satisfaction.

There's more to happiness than money, of course. And it's relative: What might be seen as having enough money for one person may not feel anywhere near enough for another person. How much do you need to feel more comfortable and secure about your financial future?

In his highly successful book, *The Secret Language of Money*, Dr. David Krueger offers a quiz in which he asks two simple questions:

1) **What is your current annual income?**

2) **In order to ensure happiness and contentment financially, with no more money problems and worries, how much annual income would you need?**

Dr. Krueger reports that in more than 9 out of 10 cases people respond that, for them to feel happy, content, and free from money worries, their annual income would need to be about twice what its current level is.

bff challenge question:

So what do you think? How much money will make you happy? Is it twice what you're making today?
Why or why not?

_____

_____

_____

_____

_____

_____

_____

_____

_____

_____

_____

_____

_____

_____

_____

For my part, I wanted the freedom to stay at home, raise my children, take care of my family and enjoy my life! The recent downturn in the economy, however, left me wanting more: a better lifestyle, more opportunities for my kids, and, call it crazy, a few luxuries! But I'd been retired from my former profession—a professional figure skater and instructor—for fourteen years! I had three young kids in tow. To tell you the truth, I wasn't too keen on stepping back on the very cold ice. And when I looked at the job opportunities available at the time, they didn't wash too well with the meager wages being offered.

Think about it. Exchanging an hour for dollars will get you nowhere, fast. Exchanging an hour for a very few dollars is just, well, depressing to say the least!

In my own case, I was frustrated, concerned, and didn't know where else to look. It was at that rock-bottom moment of my life, however, that my husband ran across a network marketing opportunity online. Little did I know that it would change my life and turn into my BFF!

If you've got teenagers, or have watched any television over the past few years, you'll know that BFF refers to a texting abbreviation for Best Friend Forever. It's used to describe a close and unshakeable friendship between two women. And the term was even co-opted by Paris Hilton for one of her shows!

The New BFF—Being Financially Free—is my way of describing the power of a relationship—a friendship—with money based on the concept of residual income. Residual income is the kind of income that fulfills dreams, which is exactly what is possible through the concept of network marketing.

Being financially free, for me, is having residual income (my paycheck arrives every 30 days, from work already done) that is greater than all of my expenses. Residual income is money I keep making from having done previous work, without having to do anything new to earn it.

What that means, essentially, is that you can live indefinitely without having to work more hours to pay your expenses. If you can understand this concept, and set it as your goal, you are one step closer to being free for life and never having to have a traditional job again.

You may or may not have heard about the network marketing business model, aka direct selling, or how it works. But network marketing can generate residual income that can result in you being financially free—BFF.

For instance, residual income pays you while attending your daughter's dance recital. It pays you while volunteering at your kids' school. It pays you while shopping, or going out to dinner, or lying on a beach in some paradise of your choosing. Residual income can arrive every week, two weeks, or thirty days (depending on your company), rain or shine, in sickness or in health! Sound too good to be true? Nope! It's going to become your new BFF! In my case, and in the case of thousands of others just like me (and maybe, you!), after a mere twelve months I didn't recognize my own life due to the financial freedom my residual income provided.

bff challenge question:

What are the first three things you would do if you had enough money, things you can't do now but wish you could?
Give details! Be specific!

_____

_____

_____

_____

_____

_____

_____

_____

_____

_____

_____

_____

_____

_____

I discovered that network marketing is a proven, solid business model that combines networking and word-of-mouth marketing. Networking is one of life's most important skills. I think entire college courses should be devoted to it! It's something we do all the time whether we're intentional about it or not. Word-of-mouth marketing is another skill we have and use every day, again, either intentionally or not. How often do you do or try or buy something one of your friends or co-workers suggested? One of the things that makes network marketing so special and powerful is that it is based on historically proven entrepreneurial techniques, and on skills all women already possess!

In other words, you can be successful working from home and doing what you already do: being yourself, being a great mom, romancing your significant other, having fun with your girlfriends. An added benefit is also knowing that you don't have to call-off from work or explain any of it to a boss. *Your schedule is your own.* BFF provides a lifestyle. It's your life to enjoy exactly as your heart desires, all the while getting paid.

I bet the idea of working from home, staying closer to your children, and earning unlimited residual income has piqued your interest at this point. Why wouldn't it? I should tell you now, however, that this is a part-time gig for 95 percent of people who get involved. So no one is telling you to run out and quit your job just yet! We all have bills to pay and responsibilities to uphold. But the great thing is that if you work hard at it part time, eventually you may decide to walk away from your job and build your residual wealth in part-time hours.

Based on my experience, I know that there are probably many other thoughts running through your head right now, like, "I'm not qualified" or "I didn't go to college" or "I've been out of the workplace too long" or "It isn't cost efficient to work outside of the home" or "I'm a single mother who can't afford to quit my job."

These types of thoughts and self-doubts are commonplace, especially for working women and stay-at-home mothers, even though the thoughts are completely false. It is these false beliefs or thoughts that keep the average woman plugging along day after day, week after week, year after year, trying to get ahead by exchanging precious hours she'd rather be spending at home or with her children for an hourly wage and specific hours dictated by someone else doing

natalia's action tip:

It's important to be strong—even a bit selfish—about your goals and dreams. Keeping your focus clear and your attitude positive is crucial to maintaining energy and momentum. My rule of thumb is: Don't allow energy sappers (aka negative people) to invade your three-foot zone of personal space!

the same thing. You spend years trying to prove yourself enough to the higher ups to "deserve" a raise, some extra time off, or some other reward. Why?

bff challenge question:

If you're a working woman, are you getting paid what you're worth? What "ends" are you working towards? Why? If you're a stay-at-home mom, what benefits would being an entrepreneur afford you?

_____

_____

_____

_____

_____

_____

_____

_____

_____

_____

_____

_____

_____

_____

_____

_____

_____

Sure, a lot people make ends meet working for others, if every-thing goes smoothly. However, life doesn't always go smoothly. Life happens on life's terms: illness, getting laid off or having your job outsourced to India, car problems, no raise again this year, braces for the kids, college tuition, the washer goes on the fritz, aging parents need help, and more. It's always the unexpected life events that push us out of control and keep the ends from meeting. And it is typically the women, the mothers, and the homemakers who juggle all the necessary components in an effort to make ends meet—and women who are left to worry, feel guilty, and make sacrifices.

If you're a single parent, a stay-at-home mom in this two-income society, or are working along with your spouse or partner to make ends meet, money worries are inevitably forcing heartbreaking sacri-fices and no-win decisions. You end up not being able to contribute to your child's college education, or telling your child you can't afford that soccer camp, or skipping your own dental appointments this year so your kid can have braces. It can be hard to imagine financial freedom when you're continually stressed out by choices that don't seem to have an upside.

For working moms, every decision seems to be plagued by "mother's guilt:" Do you stay at home with your sick child or finish the project at

natalia's action tip:

Rather than ask, "Why me?," hold on to a "Why not me?" attitude for success! I love this quote by Donny Deutsch, from his book, *Often Wrong, Never in Doubt:* "The key to success is not purely who's the smartest, who's the best, but also who can say with conviction, 'I deserve it.' The entire concept is wrapped up in one phrase: 'Why not me?'"

work with the always-urgent deadline; or pick up your child late from daycare and grab fast food for dinner due to work demands; or miss your child's sixth birthday because you had to attend a business conference? In my experience, it is painfully evident that financial worry, guilt, and sacrifice are like incessantly bad weather. They erode your mood, limit your decisions and opportunities, separate you from others, keep you from enjoying the moment, and prevent you from doing what you truly want to do.

So, instead of just trying to make ends meet, imagine that all necessary income, time flexibility, and freedom are at your disposal, ready to handle whatever may arise. BFF permits that level of ease with life's inevitable storms! You make great money while you are busy living the life you dreamed of regardless of what gets thrown at you. BFF is your opportunity to take control, increase your choices, and de-stress your life. "Why not you?" Ready? Let's go!

bff challenge question:

If you could create your dream life and schedule, what are the top three characteristics—what would it look like? Add any details or notes to yourself that will help you form a clear picture. At the end, write, "I am going to make this happen by building a successful home-based business."

_____

_____

_____

_____

_____

_____

_____

_____

_____

_____

_____

_____

_____

_____

_____

_____

chapter

you, an entrepreneur? "why not?"

"You need to dig, people! What is it that drives you deep within? You may find that it has nothing to do with money. Search your heart. Tell your mind to shut up! This is where you will find your answer and discover your WHY."

SIMON SINEK, *Start with Why*

Let's face it, for some of us, the idea of striking out on our own in business is, well, terrifying! What's neat about network marketing is that, on many levels, you're in charge of your destiny—but you're not alone. We've discussed the benefits of working from home and being financially free, so now let's look at what it means to be a network marketing entrepreneur.

This profession allows women to develop their character and grow their leadership, business and people skills. I found this benefit to be priceless since I started with no business experience, no corporate background, no writing experience, no income, no business-building credibility, and few contacts!

bff challenge question:

Recently, the *Direct Selling News* published a ten-page spread in *USA Today* with the title of *The Original Social Business Model.* It included lots of research, tips and articles for entrepreneurs. One article was entitled, "7 Reasons Why You Should Be an Entrepreneur." I wanted to share with you the seven reasons the author, K. Shelby Skrhak, gave for why network marketing is such a great business model. Are any of these important to you?

1. Job Security

Only a generation or two ago, going into business for yourself was considered risky, and the safest route was to get a good job in a large firm. "That's what my 'poor dad' taught me," says *Rich Dad, Poor Dad* author Robert Kiyosaki. "Now, working for a traditional corporation has become the risky option."

2. Make More Money

A U.S. Federal Reserve survey shows the average household net worth for entrepreneurs is five times more than that of the traditionally employed. What that means in this economy is business owners are five times more likely to come out of the recession in the black because they created income in their own businesses.

3. Freedom

When you are your own boss, you get to choose when you work, how you work, and with whom you work. Best-selling author, radio host and wealth expert, Dave Ramsey, puts it this way: "There's been a lot of doom and gloom in the media this year. The truth is, many people were laid off from jobs they hated anyway. Many people, instead of sitting home and sulking, have used the freedom to think about what they really want to do when they grow up. You have ideas—go do it!"

4. Discover Your Hidden Potential

"Entrepreneurship is business's beating heart," says Virgin mogul Richard Branson. "Entrepreneurship isn't about capital; it's about ideas. Entrepreneurship is also about excellence. Not excellence measured in awards or other people's approval, but the sort that one achieves for oneself by exploring what the world has to offer."

5. A Second Career

The nation's 78 million baby boomers are just starting to reach retirement age, yet they're realizing that they can't afford to retire. What's more, they don't want to. Dr. Mary Furlong, author of *Turning Silver into Gold*, says, "Boomers are looking for ways to give back. They are taking the reins of their own futures and redefining their lives. They want

work that reflects their values and identity; they want to make a difference." A landmark study by MetLife Foundation and Civic Ventures
found that 50 percent of Americans in their 50s and 60s want to do
work "that matters."

6. You're Sharing, Not Selling

"It turns out [direct selling] may be the best way to sell goods in
the developing world where people listen to testimonials—not
advertisements and retail sales people," Jim Cramer, host of CNBC's
Mad Money, told his audience.

7. A Life of Greater Impact

"When you're in business for yourself, you write your own history,
you write your own success story, you write your own legacy and
most important, you write your own paycheck," says Jeffrey Gitomer,
best-selling author of *Little Red Book of Selling*. "Being in business
for yourself gives you the opportunity to work your heart out for
something you love."

(September, 2011, *Direct Selling News* insert in *USA Today* titled *The Original Social
Business Model* – Article by K. Shelby Skrhak, "Why You Should Be an Entrepreneur")

Take a look at the first word in the term *network marketing*. As
I'm sure you're aware, in business, a network is an arrangement of
people who share vision, goals, enthusiasm and success. It is based
on communication and mutual benefit; their combined efforts are
connected for a common purpose.

Network marketing is simply a business model. It's a method
of marketing and distribution that's a little different than your

average retail setup. The products tend to be unique, and instead of the company spending large sums of money on advertising, hiring celebrity endorsers, and filling retail shelf space, they compensate their distributors for product sales and for building an organization of like-minded distributors.

If you have ever been to an Apple Computer or IKEA© furniture store, you'll know exactly what I mean. A store should be a place where people want to go because they enjoy a great experience. It isn't just the great products they sell that make it successful, it's the total store experience. IKEA doesn't miss a chance to enhance the customer experience, from the contemporary store design to in-store restaurants to their customer-friendly room themes.

This in turns leads to a free—but powerful—word-of-mouth marketing campaign. All it takes is one consumer recommendation for the domino effect to kick in. Have you ever heard anyone say that they love their "Mac" computer and wonder aloud why everyone doesn't use one? FYI, recently Apple became the largest company in the world with $100 billion in cash in its till!

And then there's Facebook. Way back in 2004, when they officially launched their online social media platform, they gave the world the ability to re-engage old friends and contacts and easily make new ones. It spread via the power of word-of-mouth marketing: "One person told two friends. And they told two friends. And they told two friends. And so on, and so on and so on." According to the latest data, there are over 500 million active users. Wow! People-to-people service and marketing is a powerful way of gaining momentum!

Network marketing works basically the same way, through relationship referrals, or "word-of-mouth." At its essence is the one-to-one relationship between two people that gets multiplied each time those people connect with other people. You talk to a girlfriend, and she talks to a girlfriend, and so on down the line. The key is that each person you talk to—who joins your network—creates residual income for you, for them, and potentially each person down that line also creates income for you. And it's residual income that is the basis of BFF, and the foundation of your new business. Yes, you're sharing appreciation for a product, like a skincare line, for example. But ultimately what you're sharing with those other women is how to be financially free! And trust me, if you are financially free, you can spend your money on beautifying your entire life, not just your hair or your skin or your wardrobe!

And let's face it, whether it is a new shampoo we've tried or the latest movie or a cute sweater on sale, women share things they like (and don't like) with other women. We share what works and what doesn't. We share what's hip and trendy and what's yesterday's has-been. We share feelings, insights, information, and products. It's in our DNA. We're communicators, and we do it naturally. Twice as many women as men are starting businesses right now. Women are online and hanging out in social media sites like Facebook 30 percent more than men. The Direct Selling Association (DSA) states that 82 percent of network marketing and direct sales businesses are owned by women! We're nurturing, supportive, down to earth and great communicators. So why not get paid for it? The key to BFF is that you get paid for sharing.

Network marketing compensates you to converse and socialize, to share products and share opportunities. In other words, you get paid for being you. Through social media sites like Facebook and LinkedIn®, people are harnessing the power of word-of-mouth marketing and networking because it is the strongest and most effective way to create opportunities, land a new job, or build up one's contact list. Word of mouth works. Its credibility and reliability have been proven time and again since people first started bartering and trading and selling and buying. What's most encouraging in our age of instant communication is that business analysts predict word-of-mouth marketing—the key to the multi-billion dollar network marketing industry—will become even more effective and powerful due to how quickly we share information. Word of mouth's credibility lies in trust, and trust is greatest at the level of one-to-one contact.

At its most basic level, BFF starts with a social gathering, whether planned or impromptu. Your business is built upon relationships—business partnerships, really—developed in small groups, and in one-on-one chats with neighbors or friends or fellow soccer moms or fellow shoppers. Many of my best business

natalia's action tip:

Every day when I leave my house, I'm excited to discover who will come into my life on that day. Anyone I meet when I'm out and about will hear about my business, and I'm always looking for savvy people to join my team. How do I get them engaged? Simply by talking with them, by being me.

partners have resulted from a coffee meeting at Starbucks® (one of my many offices!). These informal meetings involve talking and sharing about great products and a great business opportunity—just sharing, never selling. I'm not a salesperson. I don't want or need to try and convince someone to buy something they don't want or need.

What I love is to talk about things that are important to me. I always have. So I found a product and company that I am passionate about, I shared it with others, and, utilizing a networking business model, I am now financially free. The results are undeniable. Within six months of starting my business, I was generating a six-figure annual residual income, and it has gone up dramatically every year since then.

In 2012, I achieved my company's Million Dollar Circle. Yes, in three and a half years I went from a stay-at-home mom earning zero dollars, to a "mompreneur" who earned over one million dollars. In 2013, I will become a million-dollar-a-*year* earner! Now *that* is exciting! My hope for you is that you are motivated to truly own your life, and to become financially free in the process.

It was not luck or chance that generated that level of income. It was my desire for something more. And guess what? You can have more, too. You can truly have it all!

Here's a happy note of caution, however: Networking is not an isolating, lonely endeavor. It takes teamwork. The better the team, the more players and word of mouth, the more potential wealth for all. I talk more about building your team in Chapter Seven, but for now I just want you to realize that you will not be alone on the path to being financially free!

bff challenge question:

Are you ready to be an entrepreneur?
Here are the 10 essential characteristics you will need to become a successful network marketer. Circle the number that corresponds with how much of each you possess (1 is weakest and 10 is strongest):

I Desire Financial Freedom	1 2 3 4 5 6 7 8 9 10
I Am Disciplined	1 2 3 4 5 6 7 8 9 10
I Enjoy Making Commitments	1 2 3 4 5 6 7 8 9 10
I Am Accountable	1 2 3 4 5 6 7 8 9 10
I Have Self-Confidence	1 2 3 4 5 6 7 8 9 10
I Am Self-Motivated	1 2 3 4 5 6 7 8 9 10
I Am Coachable	1 2 3 4 5 6 7 8 9 10
I Embrace the Chance to Lead	1 2 3 4 5 6 7 8 9 10
I Am Resilient	1 2 3 4 5 6 7 8 9 10
I Set and Achieve Goals	1 2 3 4 5 6 7 8 9 10

Now, add up your scores. If you scored 50 or higher, you are primed for this business! One major key to this exercise is what you circled for "I Desire Financial Freedom." Hopefully, you ranked it as an 8 or higher. Why? Well, because it is probably your strongest answer to, "Why?"

What do I mean? Well, why would you do this? Why would you try something new? Why would you devote your future to a relatively unknown effort? Why would you make that call, schedule that appointment, attend that meeting, talk to that stranger? We are driven to succeed by strongly and confidently answering our "Why?" It must be compelling. My "why" is my three beautiful children. I am reminded every day when I see their smiling faces why I'm in this business. My "why" is what keeps me going and motivated each and every day of my life. Without a strong "why" you may not follow through, and besides, all the rest can be learned or improved over time. Your "why" can't really be learned. It needs to be there, a part of you from the beginning, strong and pesky and unshakeable. A hunger for financial freedom—and all that means to you—is a very compelling "Why."

The quietly courageous Rosa Parks was quoted as saying, "When that white driver stepped back toward us, when he waved his hand and ordered us up and out of our seats, I felt a determination that covered my body like a quilt on a winter night." She also said, "I had no idea when I refused to give up my seat on that Montgomery bus that my small action would help put an end to the segregation laws in the south. I only knew that I was tired of being pushed around. I was a regular person, just as good as anybody else."

All women possess the ability to manifest a "Why?" so strong that nothing will stand in their way, but it's up to you to be as determined as Rosa Parks was. When I think about determination, I also like to recall the words of Mary Morrissey: "Even though you may want to move forward in your life, you may have one foot on the brakes.

In order to be free, we must learn how to let go. Release the hurt. Release the fear. Refuse to entertain your old pain. The energy it takes to hang onto the past is holding you back from a new life. What is it you would let go of today?"

These traits and mindsets are implemented every day by women just like yourself as we go about our busy lives. Network marketing doesn't ask any more of you than to be yourself. And it pays you for another thing you're already an expert at doing: multi-tasking! See, you are an excellent entrepreneur, just like me. And just like I used to be, you just don't know it, yet. And one thing's for sure: You haven't started getting paid what you're worth! I hope you believe in yourself enough to get started. I sure do!

To paraphrase something motivational guru Tony Robbins says quite frequently, people don't act because they associate more pain with action than with doing nothing. So true! If you think that doing something will cause you pain, especially if you think that pain will go on and on, you might as well forget it.

Naturally, if you think a change will bring you joy and happiness, you're more likely to go after it. My husband experienced this very phenomenon about one year ago. He hadn't been to a doctor for a checkup in years. Being over 40, one day he decided it would be a good idea to get a physical. At the doctor's office, he was weighed in and had his blood pressure taken. Lo and behold, he had elevated blood pressure and had gained more than 30 pounds over the years. Told his weight, he was in disbelief. He even went as far as to have the doctor re-check his weight without his shoes, LOL! Same results. Being told what his proper weight range should be for a man his age and height set off his "Aha Moment!" He came home and announced that he was no longer willing to be that controlled by food. He announced he was already "skinny in his mind." This is important because he now associated more pleasure with being healthy than unhealthy. He has never taken a step backwards after making that affirmation.

If you want it badly enough, you'll do it. How badly do you want to be financially free?

bff challenge question:

Let's assume that being financially free is a good thing, and that it's something you're hungry for. Think for a bit about what being financially free would mean for you. How would it change your life in ways that are important to you now? How would it impact your—and your family's—future? Be specific.

_____

_____

_____

_____

_____

_____

_____

_____

_____

_____

_____

_____

_____

_____

_____

natalia's action tip:

I'm going to suggest that you keep this book, and your answers to the challenge questions like the one above, near at hand and available as you go forward toward BFF. If you encounter challenges or obstacles that seem too much to overcome, or if you get tired or feel lazy or just need a jumpstart, come back to these questions and answers as inspiration and motivation for your efforts. You can be a successful entrepreneur, you can build a great team, you can do anything your business requires for success. Why? Because you want to be financially free, with all that means to you!

chapter

natalia's little secret

"The big secret in life is that there is no big secret. Whatever your goal, you can get there if you're willing to work."

OPRAH WINFREY

By now, most of you have heard of the bestselling book, *The Secret*. Based on the Law of Attraction™, the idea is that if you think and believe something will come to you, the universe will give it to you. Well, I'm all for thinking positively—you usually can't get something if you don't think you can—but my secret involves a little more action and a little less waiting for the universe!

Yes, I want to live my dreams. Yes, I want financial freedom. Yes, I want to stay home with my kids and have fun doing it. Okay, now how do I make that happen?

My jumpstart was learning about a network marketing opportunity with a young, California-based skin care company a mere three years ago. The opportunity would allow me to work part-time, from home, and potentially make $500, or $5,000, or $10,000, or even $50,000 or more a month! My kids were users of their other highly successful products (which are advertised on television, and you've probably seen their ads), and I knew people loved and trusted the company founders, so I knew they were the real deal. I also knew that, if I had the chance to partner with them on their next big business venture, I would take it. After looking into the opportunity, I knew two more things: I was willing to do the work, and I loved the idea of BFF!

There are a few things you should know about me. No, I don't have a business degree, and I had absolutely zero network marketing experience. I haven't tried to climb the corporate ladder or break the perpetual glass ceiling in a company or industry. For the last fourteen years, I've stayed at home to raise my three adorable children, and before that I taught figure skating. What I'm getting at is that I am not exactly the quintessential model of a businesswoman, even though I knew I had the discipline and an undeniable entrepreneurial spirit. I was and still am a devoted mom to my children, Daphne, Hunter, and Scarlett, first and foremost. And today, I'm not only a stay-at-home mom, but a stay-at-home mompreneur success story to boot!

On the other hand, what I have always had is a willingness to roll up my sleeves and sink my teeth into any project to get the job done, a can-do spirit, and the gift of gab. I know those are qualities I share with huge numbers of women, probably even you! After all, isn't that exactly what it takes to be a stay-at-home mom, a single workingwoman juggling it all alone, or, more simply put, a woman in our society today? We don't get the luxury of ignoring a ringing phone, a crying child, a demanding boss, an aging parent needing our help, or even a hungry spouse. From the time we are born, we learn to take charge and juggle whatever life happens to throw at us, all the while engaging others and chatting and listening along the way.

It is that very tenacity and ability to connect with and support others that qualifies you and me for this business model that has so dramatically changed my life. And you can change yours, too, for the better and for good.

You have all the skills, qualifications, education, and experience, *right now*, to become financially free. You definitely don't have to wait for your kids to leave home, move to a different city, go back to school, or wait another minute to live your wildest dreams. Believe me, who you are, right now, is the perfect background for success in this business model.

Whatever your experiences have been up until now, you will draw off of them, as I have, and apply what you've learned towards your goal of being a networking entrepreneur. My skating years, for example, taught me persistence and a strong work ethic. When all my teenage friends were sleeping in before school, I was at the rink practicing. No, I didn't go on to be an Olympic or World Champion, but I skated side-by-side with those that did, which made me a better skater. Apparently, I wasn't meant to an Olympian, but a passion and love for skating, coupled with working and competing within such a winning environment, made all of us better skaters—and better women. And it was exhilarating! Still, I trusted there was something bigger ahead of me; I just didn't know what or where to find it. So I attended college until the opportunity to professionally teach skating presented itself. I jumped at the chance to follow my heart, which I thought at the time meant only my love of skating.

But lo and behold, I found another love, too. I met the man I was going to marry! And that taught me lessons and opened new opportunities. First and foremost, a few short years later, I embraced my biggest opportunity of all: motherhood. Motherhood has been and continues to be my greatest joy in life and my biggest learning opportunity. And it has directly translated into my business. What I have learned about prioritization, multi-tasking, teamwork, organization, communication, community, and of course connectivity and passion, I've learned from being a mother.

Motherhood and all my other former, non-standard, professional experiences are the very reasons my dynamic team and I are one of the top producers within my company. Within the first 24 months of launching my business, BFF allowed my husband and I to travel to exotic places like The Four Seasons in Maui and Las Ventanas, in Los Cabos, where the rich and famous go to play. My BFF has enabled me to pay for my daughter's competitive dance travel expenses, hire a seasoned saxophone musician for private lessons in my home for my son, pay for the college of choice for my eldest daughter, and of course aggressively invest in and solidify my family's financial future.

As a stay-at-home mother, I know my contribution is invaluable to our family and its financial well-being. However, to be able to ac- tually contribute such a high level of income for our financial future is something I never imagined I could do, and something I am most proud of, especially without having to sacrifice seeing my children grow up.

Another perk of my business is the ability to earn various incentives and rewards often offered by companies within our business model. For instance, I drive a brand new, super-cute, luxury convertible that I earned by building such a remarkably talented and driven team. The free vehicle is only one of the many types of incentives. I also get numerous, free (fully paid for), exotic vacations yearly. Our company also has a generous override bonus for qualified, top tier distributors that adds big money to my income. This override alone covers our mortgage and all of our other monthly bills! These types of awards and rewards are not only fun and exciting to earn, but they add to our family's financial portfolio. Hey, we no longer have a car payment! And a free car is a fun car!

No big deal? Everyone has a car payment, right? Hold on a minute. Think about what your life would be like with an extra $500 to $1,000 every month for the rest of your life. It's no wonder people can't retire! I read somewhere that by saving $500 a month for a year, and then adding $100 a month to that each year (next year it's $600 a month, the year after that its $700 a month, and so on), over just 20 years, you'd have $1 million. Would that help your family? And all that from just saving your car payment! Now imagine being able to save 20 percent of your yearly income as well. I was an avid Oprah watcher and can recall her having Suze Orman as a guest on her show. What resonated most with me was Suze's plea for us to get the same amount of pleasure from saving money as from perpetually shopping. Mind you, I love shopping, but it feels amazing to build up my nest egg every month.

Hopefully, it has become obvious that BFF means income unlimited enough to control your own destiny and do just about anything you can imagine. But here's the truth: The one "freedom" my stellar income hand delivers to me each and every moment is freedom from worry. Today, I am free from that energy sucker and that, my friend, is priceless.

And that's my little "secret!" BFF affords me the time, energy, mental space and financial security to live the dream life. But the best part is, when I wake up each day, the dream is real, and starts all over again. And it can for you, too.

bff challenge question:

Are you stressed out over money and work? How much of an impact has lack of financial freedom had on your emotional well-being? Your marriage or relationships? Describe your frustrations and concerns.

_____

_____

_____

_____

_____

_____

_____

_____

_____

_____

_____

_____

_____

_____

_____

_____

chapter

leverage

"Time is wealth, and unlike money, when it is gone,
you cannot replace it."

NAPOLEON HILL

You've probably heard the term "leverage" used in various ways. In its purest form, a lever is a tool to give you a mechanical advantage in doing work. It's the ability to control a lot with minimum effort, and to have more power than you would all by yourself. Through leverage, you can create financial change more quickly. The more leverage you have, the faster you can accumulate wealth.

In the world of high finance, leverage is using credit or borrowing to gain advantage in speculating on investments. But what I'm referring to here is "our female advantage," or, to be more blunt, "girlfriend power."

Here's a general example. Men frequently leverage golf as a business-to-business relationship builder and deal enhancer. In my world, I leverage Starbucks! Why? Starbucks serves some of the best coffee in the world, and brings a lot of happiness into our lives. Starbucks effectively coined the concept of "the third place," defined as a place for people to meet and socialize away from home and work. Many of us flock there every day to network and socialize with our smart and savvy girlfriends. Through just this one medium, you can become connected to a tremendous number of people. Through my new BFF lifestyle, I now "combine and conquer" by using it as my virtual office (and with all the Starbucks locations, I have a lot of offices). It's like having a fully functional mobile office wherever you go. Plus, I hear they are possibly planning to test market serving wine in certain California locations. So now there may be another way to leverage Starbucks: Happy Hour!

In terms of making a living, BFF is all about leveraging key tools: time, money, and resources. In doing so, it offers maximum short-term rewards while also ensuring long-term financial freedom to pursue any and all of your desired goals. Don't think for a minute that only men can take advantage of leverage. Women are natural-born networkers. Combine that with the social media revolution, the ease of global connectivity, and the fact that women now run about 70 percent of home-based businesses, and it's undeniable. Leverage is even more powerful in a woman's hands!

Here's an example. When I joined my company it cost me just under $1,000. By the end of the first month, I had earned my in-vestment back, PLUS had enough reserve funds to run my business expense-free for the next six months. This was only made possible through the leverage of having 20 to 30 people join my team, all working toward similar goals. Typically, when you buy a business or franchise, it will take you three to five years just to recover your initial investment. It wasn't magic or luck or my sheer brilliance. It was the leverage offered through the network marketing business model.

What's most exciting about network marketing is that it is a relationship-building business. Its greatest resource—and yours—is people. You build a great team of people whose time, talent, experience and enthusiasm multiply the power of your efforts exponentially. And it does so for all the tools you have at your disposal: time, money and resources. Let's take a closer look at how this works.

Since you probably wouldn't be reading this book unless you were interested in financial change, let's start there. When you bring your first business partner into your network, you've grown your team—and leverage power—by 100%. If you and she sponsor one new person each, the network is four. Each of them does the same for a total of eight. Even if each of the eight only sponsors one person, you're now at sixteen networkers. Each of them connects with one person, and if each of them does the same you're now at sixty four people in your "down-line." So far, you have talked to six people. Now, all of you chat with one person, and your network consists of 128 people, with your actual number of contacts having been just seven people! The leverage of financially gaining from other people's resources and desires is what primarily differentiates network marketing from a standard job.

Network marketing also offers residual income, while a standard job offers linear income. With a standard job, you are compensated once for your efforts (hourly, salary, or unit of production/piecework). I love what poet Robert Frost has to say about employment: "By working faithfully eight hours a day you may eventually get to be boss and work twelve hours a day."

The two main drawbacks of linear income from a standard job are:

1) Your earning is capped, or limited, ahead of time, based on your hours or production.

You're trading hours for dollars. No matter how well you perform at your job for a big box retailer, your request to go from $10/hour to $50/hour will be denied at your annual review! By contrast, one of my good friends in my company went from working for a retail wage to a being a millionaire in less than three years.

2) If you stop working, you stop earning.

Even a doctor with all his or her education and training must show up to get paid! My good friend and business partner's husband is a successful doctor. What's her reason for doing this business? She wants to replace her husband's great income, so when he decides to retire, they will be able to continue their lifestyle. Now, in less than two years, she is knocking on the door of a six-figure residual income and has the company's free luxury car.

So even at the upper echelons of salaried professions, yes, you can earn a great living, but it's still a one-off arrangement based solely on your presence. Even then your position or company could be eliminated without notice. One of my personal favorite business partners was fired from her company after 25 years as one of their top sales performers. She was responsible for landing one of her company's biggest accounts. She was called into a meeting one day with the thought that she would be getting a raise. After a few minutes into the meeting it became clear that she was being let go due to cost cutting. Not to be deterred, she joined my organization at the age of 62 and in three years has more than doubled her 25-year career income.

With network marketing there is no maximum threshold on your income. The efforts of others assist in helping you build your business and team. The more people and the more sharing, the more potential wealth generated for all. When your team makes money, you make money. The bigger your team, the more potential. The combined efforts of you and your team create unlimited income potential. No thresholds. No caps!

natalia's action tip:

The only time I'm "Closed for Business" is when I'm sleeping, and even then I'm still making money! A few power partners on your team, committed to building big, can give birth to a fortune in residual income for you. Sir Isaac Newton's First Law of Motion states, "An object at rest tends to stay at rest, and an object in motion tends to stay in motion." You are the one who keeps the motion going forward in your business by leading by example!

And I love the leverage of residual income. If you stop working—or happen to get sick, or want to take the day or week off to be with family, or take a real vacation—you still make money. Leveraging the money-making power of residual income means financial freedom now and into the future.

The second source of leverage in network marketing is time. Goodness knows, there never seems to be enough of it to go around! The early 21st century is marked and marred by time poverty. Ridiculous and perpetual demands on our time create stress and frustration unknown to many previous generations. Working women, especially working moms, know this all too well. It feels like life flies by in the blink of an eye! I clearly remember being on the ice at fifteen years old all worried about whether I was going to land all my scheduled double jumps in competition. It's hard to get my head around the idea that it was a quarter of a century ago!

While I can't change the number of hours in a day, or the number of days in a week, I can assure you that network marketing helps you "buy" time by creating efficiencies in how you make money.

Let's take a look at the average working person who's on the job five days a week, or 40 hours, for 50 weeks a year (assuming you get two weeks vacation!). That's 2,000 hours a year, or 80,000 of work time over a 40 year career. Sounds like a lot, but is it really?

In network marketing, let's say you worked your business hard for a number of years like I have, and you built a massive team of 10,000 people. Now let's say they all work for just ONE eight-hour day. That's 80,000 hours in ONE DAY, the same amount it takes you a lifetime to work. You couldn't begin to match this leverage on your own.

Take a moment to think about this example: Picture the school teacher, who admirably goes to school each day, with the vital and under-appreciated task of educating our children. Let's say the average teacher makes $40,000 a year. Over the next 10 years of her life, the teacher will have earned about $400,000 worth of income. This is where the power of networking is clear as a school bell. I myself make more in 12 months than that teacher will make in the next 10 years of her life. In just over three years of working my business, I'll earn as much as the teacher who works her entire 30-year career.

One of my close friends and business partners is a now-retired (she was working full time before we met) school teacher from Knoxville, TN. Her story was that she was simply looking for good skincare for her son. One day, one of her friends asked her what she was up to, so she shared her story. To her surprise, her friend said, "Do you know what a great opportunity you have with this company?"

Here's another way of looking at how network marketing helps you leverage time:

Daily Hours:

Because you *and* your team, rather than you alone, create the distribution of product or services, less of your individual daily hours are committed to earning income. This leaves you more quality time to spend with your significant others, all the while still getting paid.

Yearly Hours:

Yearly hours leverage in a similar fashion. The larger your team, the larger the distribution, the greater the wealth potential. Substantial residual income can be produced relatively quickly—especially compared with linear job income. In a standard job there is no residual income per se. You can, of course, invest some of your income from a standard job, but we all know that it takes large investments, lots of time, and a fair amount of luck to become financially free that way. With network marketing, achieving time and financial freedom not only creates a solid financial future, it allows you to live and enjoy the life you have always dreamed of much sooner!

Residual Hours:

Residual income creates residual hours. Whether you choose to increase your work efforts, slow them down, or stop them when and if you decide to retire, residual income arrives into your mailbox every month, regardless of what you do today or tomorrow. So whether you want to go in a new direction, or retire, or spend your newfound free time in any number of exciting ways, you still get paid. No, residual income can't buy you happiness, but it can buy you the freedom of time to live your life to the fullest. What you do with your time is up to you, but, from my perspective, nothing has made me happier than creating that freedom for my family and myself. It's a gift that keeps on giving, and I am truly thankful for it.

Last, but certainly not least, is the power of leveraging resources I touched on in my Starbucks example. A major advantage of network marketing over standard employment is the exponential strength of teamwork. Let's look at how it works.

Let's say you designed websites for a living. You charge $1,000 per site, and you can do about two per week. But if you were able to find 10 people to do two websites per week, look what happens. You charge $1,000, pay the others $800, and make $4,000 per week instead of $2,000. You leveraged a resource (other people's skill) to exponentially increase your income. Yes, you put in some time (more leverage) to get jobs and find designers, but you're putting in zero extra time designing websites and making twice as much money by leveraging the efforts of others.

In the case of network marketing, you're teaching your team to duplicate your efforts. The more people you have duplicating, the more successful you'll be. It's an equal opportunity situation that encourages and rewards effort and teambuilding.

What this network marketing tip is really about is giving everybody an equal opportunity to be successful. You have the ability to earn as I do. And the more people we leverage, the more successful we can be.

And if someone isn't pulling their weight, it doesn't do as much damage as in other work. Let's say one of your website designers is sick all week. You're still making $3,600 a week, or $1,600 more than you could on your own. This is a good example of the adage, "Teamwork makes the dream work."

Teams provide the network to distribute the product, and they also provide a positive environment, which allows the best chance of success for all. *Your greatest resource is the people that make up your team.* It's like a family that supports each other and collaborates to ensure the best results for all. When you choose the right company and right team, you have immediately joined a pool of resources dedicated to the same outcome: being financially free!

I can think of no other way to make a living that leverages money, time and resources for the power to achieve financial and personal freedom. My own experiences confirm what's possible, and that's why I'm so eager to share them with you. I hope you'll leverage what you learn in this book to start enjoying the power of being financially free!

bff challenge question:

Whether you currently work at a job or not, your choices either benefit you or they don't. Now ask yourself, "Would I like to be a successful network marketing entrepreneur?" Why? Make a list of the pros and cons and choose the side that resonates within you.

_____

_____

_____

_____

_____

_____

_____

_____

_____

_____

_____

_____

_____

_____

_____

_____

chapter

choosing wisely

"Work with the willing, love the rest."

NATALIA YOSCO

The road to financial freedom starts with choosing the right company. There are many, many network marketing opportunities out there. Some are outstanding, some stand out for the wrong reasons. Your success, both in the short run and over time, depends on finding the right fit and building on a solid foundation.

Finding the right fit for you is all about passion. You must love what you do! This may seem like obvious advice, because bringing passion to your work, your hobbies, your relationships, or anything you devote your time to, improves and enhances those experiences. Yet it is especially important with network marketing. If the product or service doesn't excite you, or hold value for you personally, you're less likely to want to share it with others.

So find a product line or service that excites you. What you're looking for is a situation in which you can't wait for the next day to begin. You want a company that fits seamlessly with your personality or interests or background. If you are a shoe enthusiast, look for a company focused on shoes. If you love books and reading, look for a publishing company. If it's beauty and glamour, take a look at make-up or socially responsible clothing or even skincare. Follow your passions and interests to a company that delivers what you love. Like Willie Wonka's famous everlasting gobstoppers, you want to be satisfied forever!

For me, I've been a skincare junkie most of my life. I've spent countless hours and more money than I care to admit in pursuit of beautiful, clear, radiant skin. I've slathered and soaked, scrubbed and brushed so many products over the years that my passion for skincare primping was obvious not only to me, but to most people who knew me!

Upon moving to Nashville, I became friends with a woman who was and is married to a country music artist, is fabulous inside and out, and who also happened to be working her network marketing business with a skincare company. She was always trying to recruit me to work with her in her company, but her company was quite saturated in our area. And though I supported my girlfriend's business endeavor by becoming a product customer, I wasn't passionate enough about her opportunity to pursue building a business with her.

Through our friendship, however, I was able to take my first peak into the industry. I learned a great deal about network marketing, especially the business structure and realistic potential of being financially free. Women in my girlfriend's up-line (part of her team) were making six figures a MONTH. I could hardly believe it when she first shared this with me, but over time, it became obvious that their lifestyles and their gorgeous homes were evidence of massive success. Sure, I was blown away by the grandiose benefits my girlfriend carefully detailed about network marketing, but I wasn't passionate about that product line. It was that simple. I loved the business model, but I couldn't get excited about the company, and I knew it wasn't the right choice for me. Perhaps, in time, something more suitable would come along. After all, timing is everything.

Let me share a few words about timing. Timing is crucial in everything we do, whether it be personal or professional. As it applies to BFF, it's about seizing a product or company you are passionate about that offers the most rewarding opportunity. One huge benefit for me was the ability to get involved in the early development stage of my network marketing company before its rapid and global expansion. This is not to say anything against well-established companies with long-term track records like the one in which my girlfriend was successful. They offer financial stability and have proven track records in the marketplace.

Catching the right company, with the right products, at the right time, is like catching time in a bottle: a true gift.

It was my husband, John, who delivered my "gift" to me, and, without naming names, I would like to "pay-it-forward" to you. My network marketing experience has changed my life in so many wonderful and even unimaginable ways. I want to share this gift with you because you absolutely deserve the opportunity to live the life of financial freedom.

My company came across my husband's radar screen while he was doing research on the Internet one day. He was instantly intrigued—by the products and by the company founders—and called me into his office to share what he'd found. By the time I got to his office, his research showed a compelling opportunity that focused on the ever-growing, multi-billion dollar anti-aging market with clinically proven anti-aging, dermatological skincare regimens—quality skincare I could stand behind—a focus that sent my heart to skipping beats. Even as John tried to persuade me to do this business, he didn't realize that I already knew the business model perfectly well due to my girlfriend's pursuits. Needless to say, I was also intrigued. It was an undeniable fit, and the business's foundation and reputation were satisfyingly solid. Then there were the factors of getting in on a new product line launch with products that met a vast audience's essential needs. A great company whose products meshed with my passions, along with perfect timing, made it the perfect choice for me personally and professionally.

Here are some potentially important things to evaluate in any company you're thinking of joining:

Brand vs. Non-Brand?

I would always recommend joining an established brand, if possible, due to the unique competitive advantage (an important factor, according to Warren Buffet). Global brands immediately afford you instant credibility (The Oprah Effect). However, the downside may be a saturated marketplace, which may make building a business too difficult for some. In cases like that, look for a brand that has a new, re-defining product coming to market, or a company that is re-branding itself with new products. The product must be unique and offer to fill an important need. The upside to a new, non-branded company is the potential for their product to become an iPad-like seller where you're getting in on the ground floor from the beginning of the product's launch. As with anything new, however, there's always the possibility of failure, so do your research!

Well-Financed Companies

Look for a well-financed company with a strong business plan and long-term commitment to success. This is where finding an established company brand often works in your favor by lowering the risks. Too many under-financed companies come into the network marketing arena hoping to strike gold before they run out of money. There is a high failure rate, as it usually takes time to gain a strong foothold with any new business or brand. Overnight successes are the exception, not the rule. So if you choose to join a startup networking company, be as close to sure as possible that the founders are fully committed to the success of their company.

Products People Want

Very few network marketing companies have poor products, but they're not necessarily what people want. Look for products that people are clamoring for, and which you know to be in high demand.

Taken a step further, Seth Godin says that brilliant marketing is all about creating products that people actually want, as opposed to products they need. The more people that want the product, the faster and more naturally it will spread.

Integrity

This is critical. You have to be able to sleep at night knowing that your company founders' intentions are honorable, respectful, and decent to a fault. Your reputation is everything and will determine your ability to grow your business. Your level of integrity should always be a solid fit with the company's level of integrity. There is no gray area allowed when it comes to this. If doubts exist and you can't get straight answers from the founders, take a pass on the company and wait to choose another one in whose integrity you have no doubts. The company should be a member of the Direct Selling Association (DSA) and in good standing. It's just another sign the company is conscious of doing the right thing.

Consumer Sense

Use your common sense for consumer sense. Use the products. Talk with other consultants and consumers. Feel the customer experience. Investment guru Peter Lynch made a fortune as one of the world's great money managers by talking with his family and friends about what products were hot, and about their experiences with them. It helped with research that resulted in his investing in winning companies over and over again. He would recommend that people use their consumer senses to get a feel for the brand, which in turn helps make a more informed investment decision on the brand's potential. For instance, walk into an Apple Store (as I mentioned earlier) and experience the products, and customer and staff enthusiasm first hand. Or visit Chipotle's restaurant and see the lines of people waiting to order their food. As a consumer, do your prospective network marketing company's business plan, products and services make sense to you? Would you want to be a consultant if approached by a distributor? Trust your common sense about the product and company you are considering.

Built to Last

In a perfect world, look to join visionary founders who offer products and/or services that deliver on their purported objectives. These types of leaders will be all about building a legacy company—and that will result in a long-term residual income stream for you. There are numerous examples of these legacy companies that have been in business anywhere from 25-50 years.

Totally Transparent

A well-run and reputable network marketing company will provide transparency with respect to typical actual earnings of their distributors. You should research whether any company you are interested in joining has an Income Disclosure Statement, which reveals statistics on high, low and average earnings for the various levels of the compensation plan. Such statements should be posted on the company's website. Reviewing it will be an important step in your due diligence process when deciding whether this is the right company for you.

Great Culture

This is related to integrity, but also has a huge social component. Plus, not only do you want to feel good about your company's products and integrity, you want to feel great about the people who are part of it. They should love what they do, and it should show! From my experience, an example of a company that has developed a great corporate culture is Publix Supermarkets. The Publix employees are always smiling and happy people who go out of their way to make sure you have a great experience. A great feature of their service is that, after you check out, they walk you to your car and unload your packages to boot.

How or why is all this important? Well, for one thing, you'll be interacting with your team and your company for years. You need to feel not only comfortable doing so, but actually excited and enthusiastic about doing so.

The mere thought of being financially free is exhilarating, but you must choose wisely. Trust what you are passionate about; getting started with a company you love is key. Once you're confident about the fit, foundation, and timing of your move, jump in with enthusiasm and build the team that will help you live your dreams!

? bff challenge question:

What are you passionate about? What products or
services, based on your interests and/or experience with
them, seem like a great fit for you?

_____

_____

_____

_____

_____

_____

_____

_____

_____

_____

_____

_____

_____

a girl's best friend

*"Our success has really been based on partnerships
from the very beginning."*

BILL GATES

A famous Broadway musical song tells us that "Diamonds Are a Girl's Best Friend," but if you want to be able to afford diamonds, start with your girlfriends! Whether they're women you call friends now, or women you have yet to meet, girlfriends are one of the key resources—and benefits—of the network marketing business structure.

Start with your "warmest market," meaning friends you already know who trust and love you. This does not mean your network team will only consist of girlfriends in your life today, but it's great to start with women with whom you already have a great relationship. My success began with the list I created the night I joined my company. I thought long and hard about who I wanted to join my team. I came up with 29 names of sharp and sassy women to approach about sharing my business. One of the most important forces for your success will be finding fully committed team players, all with the exact same goal in mind. With this start, BFF becomes possible within a few years (3-5 years is a good rule of thumb). In my experience, it helps if your team members:

- ✓ Exude business savvy, have an entrepreneurial or go-getter attitude
- ✓ Enjoy new and exciting opportunities for BFF
- ✓ Are HUNGRY, those who have felt or are feeling the effects of the economic crunch or who want to reclaim the lifestyle they no longer get to enjoy!

Hunger trumps everything! It's one of the ultimate answers to "why?" Give me a smart, hungry individual, and I know they will take advantage of the opportunity at hand and create magic. That's how I started. I was hungry as well as passionate about my company's products. So I jumped in with both feet immediately and never looked back.

I felt like a million bucks from day one (it's different for everyone, but look at it as a 3-5 year business model to give you a frame of reference) because I had my top two people join me right away. Together we started to build our teams, multiplying quickly and intensely. Remember, they also started out by getting a minimum of two Power Partnerships each (four more). Then, those people started with two (eight more) and so on and so on. We had more than 100 people join us in the first three months of business.

Remember, you are not alone! You don't have to run out and sign up hundreds of people to make this work. Start with two people who are as committed as you are, who have what it takes to make it work (see Chapter 3), and who are driven by the desire to be financially free. That's been my secret sauce from day one.

Don't get lost in your fear! Keep it simple. Here are seven tips to get you started in finding your first two effective Power Partnerships. Note: These tips should apply to you *and* to your Power Partners.

natalia's action tip:

Think of two people in your "warm market" who would be brilliant at building a team. Just come up with two girlfriends, go-getters, who want to earn significant residual income working from home. They will become your "Power Partnership" and the spark that ignites your empire.

Power Partner Tip #1: Know Your "Why?"

Why are you doing this? Your "why" has to be so big and meaningful that it can make you cry. Yes, we've talked a lot about the significant residual income you can earn, but ultimately money is money, a means to an end. What freedoms will that money afford you? That's the question. For me, it's my three children. That may sound cliché, as every parent probably feels that way. But to be able to support them and offer them anything they need in life is an amazing blessing. Financial security equals emotional and mental security for me. Recently, my daughter was deciding what college to attend. At no point was money a factor for us, due to my residual income I have earned over the last three years. The feeling of being able to support my daughter's choices based on her passions and best interests, rather than what's in our bank account, is nearly indescribable. I reflect daily on my "why," and that energizes me to push through any obstacle that may come my way.

Power Partner Tip #2: Make a List

This becomes a living document. It stays with you and grows every day. When I first joined, I made a list immediately, just off the top of my head. (That list created my "million dollar organization" and still sits on my desk today, as reminder. As I said, two of the people at the top of that list did in fact become my first two Power Partners.) Trust yourself that you already know key people who will likely join your team. Even if you don't think you know the right people, trust me, you do! Your girlfriends want the same opportunity you do to live your wildest dreams!

Power Partner Tip #3: Ready, Set, GO

Go into action immediately. After making my list, I contacted each and every one of them, a few at a time, each day over a couple of weeks. Fit it into your schedule, even if only for a half an hour a day. In my first month, I had more than two dozen people on my team. Those Power Partners and I were off and running. Some new business builders feel like they can't start until they know everything. I always remind them that they don't get paid for how much they know but for how much volume their team produces. It's an *earn-as-you-learn* program, not a study program.

Power Partner Tip #4: Talk the Talk

Learn the language that is most effective when sharing your opportunity and products. Of course, you will get better over time and with more practice. However, the smoother and more informed you can sound when sharing, the faster your business will grow. It's another reason to be passionate about the product. Passion ignites the desire to know all about it and share it, and we speak most eloquently about things that are important to us. What's more, people always are attracted to confident, knowledgeable, and passionate people.

Power Partner Tip #5: Remember, It's a Business

Treat your new business like a business. I'm a big believer in setting up an action plan and then following through. Make sure it is reasonable for your schedule and lifestyle, but pushing in the beginning means bigger benefits later. Remember, work now, get paid for years to come through residual income. So, by working the business like a business, you will be rewarded for your professionalism and efforts with financial freedom.

Follow my lead! Here's my personal daily to-do list for driving my business, based on tasks: Organize-Share-Follow Up.

Each and every day you want to release what I call your personal Leverage Boomerang into the world! Throw it out every day by incorporating all the available resources you have at your disposal: direct contact, cell phone calls, social media and email. Each and every day the boomerang returns home to you looking the same. But what is actually happening behind the scenes is that it's creating your Yellow Brick Road to Being Financially Free! Why? All those little, daily actions build up to explode your business ten-fold.

MORNING— Seize Your Day. Organize. Draw up the day's agenda. Leverage your social media tools. You are OPEN for business!

NOON— Share, share, share. Grow your business by inviting and sharing in person, via cell phone, asking for referrals and using email.

NIGHT— Share some more. Conduct business presentations. Follow up! Success comes to those who stay in touch with the most people. In our business, we say, "The fortune is in the follow up!"

EVERY CHANCE I GET— I'm Networking!

Take charge of your business! Busy as we are, there's always hidden down time in our days. Allow the power of leverage to work for you by keeping the networking switch set to "ON." I know you can find the time if you want to badly enough.

Power Partner Tip #6: Be a Product of Your Product

Use it every day and share your results with everyone! My skin is often one of the selling points for my company's product. My skin. My team's skin. Everyone in the world has skin! With a little product sample carried in my bag or car, I'm ready to do business anywhere:

✓ **In line at the store**

✓ **In the stands at my kids' events**

✓ **Chitchatting with friends**

✓ **At social gatherings**

✓ **Wherever my skin goes, my business goes**

By being the product of your product, dovetailing your business into your life becomes smooth and easy rather than a chore.

Power Partner Tip #7: Never Quit

Those who don't quit win—and sometimes win big—in this business. Yes, there are discouraging conversations, or days or times when you are hearing "no" more than "yes." This can be said about almost any endeavor in life. But remember, you only need to start with two Power Partnerships to really launch yourself into financial freedom.

Once I had formed my two Power Partnerships, we created an unspoken mission statement to provide servant leadership to all who joined our team. Make no mistake: Developing team values is the single most important thing you can do right at the outset. Without fail, the best down lines are built this way. We have created a strong team culture intimately revolving around our core values.

Here are a few that we have tried to live by:

✓ **Recruit people with the same committed vision of BFF**

✓ **Keep our customers happy and appreciated**

✓ **Support our Team Members fully throughout the process**

✓ **Create ongoing win-win attitudes throughout our network**

We all share the goal of wanting to build our businesses by help-ing all achieve their goals. It's this spirit that has allowed us to grow our team to the size it is today.

The point is this: Get going and don't stop until after you've reached your destination. We didn't stop and it paid off. Sticking to a plan, holding your "why" close to your heart and never giving up—and building a great team—are the secrets to my success. I have the coolest, most diverse, and super-fabulous people on my team. They are the engine behind the vast momentum of my organiza-tion's growth. It all started with me dreaming BIG. And yet together, working hand-in-hand, we have produced a team of thousands, now nationwide and soon to be globally, and we are all dreaming BIG.

And I made it happen by relying on a something much more precious than diamonds: my team!

chapter

teambuilding 101

"Interdependent people combine their own efforts with the efforts of others to achieve their greatest success."

STEPHEN COVEY

I hope by now you've seen that BFF is well within your reach. I know you have the skills, intelligence, and experience to be successful. Only you know whether your "why" is powerful enough to move you forward, and we'll talk a bit more about that in the last chapter. But for the moment, let's assume you want financial freedom and all it affords badly enough to dive in, but that you still have some doubts about whether you could build a successful team.

If you'll indulge me for a bit, I'd like to share what I've done to live up to the adage, "Teamwork makes the dream work." It's not complicated, but there are simple things I've done that have worked beyond my wildest expectations. You'll be surprised by the lack of mystery, and hopefully you'll be fired up to try these techniques with your business.

natalia's action tip:

Spend your days building your network in person or via the phone. It can be something as easy as a coffee and a conversation at Starbucks that can change your life!

First of all, I made the decision to be successful. It has driven me to follow through on opportunities and propelled my business forward. I incorporated my business into my life (there's a term for it, called "Lifestyle Marketing") in such a way that who I am and what I do are inseparable, and it has provided me with endless business leads because I can build my team literally everywhere I go. And in this business, it's all about teambuilding.

The larger the committed team you assemble, the greater your financial freedom. Period. But what's special about this fact is that your team grows exponentially with each member that joins. Your individual effort to bring great people on board is being duplicated by all those great people you bring on board. Yes, there will be a lot of people who quit. The old 80/20 rule is alive and well when it comes to building a business. But nothing in life comes easy, so accept it and get over it! Decide to be one of the twenty-percenters!

One of my original power partners was actually a friend to both my husband and me. One of the greatest things about him was his passion for networking and his steadfast resolve to control his own destiny. He also intuitively knew the types of people we were looking for. A great team is always a blend of different types of people who bring their individual strengths into an environment of cooperation and mutual benefit.

In Chapter Two of *The Tipping Point*, Malcolm Gladwell describes three special types of people:

Connectors:

"These people who link us up with the world, who bridge Omaha and Sharon, who introduce us to our social circles—these people on whom we rely on more heavily than we realize—are Connectors, people with a very special gift of bringing people together."

Mavens:

"A Maven is a person who has information on a lot of different products or prices or places. This person likes to initiate discussions with consumers and respond to requests . . . they like to be helpers in the marketplace. They distribute coupons. They take you shopping. They go shopping for you . . . this is the person who connects people to the marketplace and has the inside scoop on the marketplace."

Salespeople:

"Mavens are data banks. They provide the message. Connectors are social glue: they spread it. But there is also a select group of people—Salesmen—with the skills to persuade us when we are unconvinced of what we are hearing, and they are as critical to the tipping of word-of-mouth epidemics as the other two groups."

Together, my power partner and I brought our respective strengths together and decided to share our business opportunity daily with the world. I came up with the idea of working out of my community's pool club house, which served as the location to which all consultants could send their best contacts to hear about the opportunity every Monday. Whether they could attend themselves or not, we would help them build. This idea of mine would change not only our lives, but the lives of many, for the better. Each Monday, we would get to that clubhouse by 10 a.m. and sometimes not leave until after 11 p.m., all the while helping people build their businesses. This venue became so popular we were eventually asked to leave due to the amount of parking congestion we were causing. Our attitude of "invite and share" became our recipe for success!

One day as I was at home upstairs, the doorbell rang and when I answered it, I saw a cute gal in a hound's tooth jacket standing outside my door. She seemed to want to chat about the new Chiropractic office in the neighborhood. Her appearance caught my attention right away. She was dressed super sharp and sported big, fun jewelry. Instantly, I knew she would be great for my business. I immediately complimented her on her style and asked her where she was from. Murfreesboro, TN, she said, which is outside of the Nashville area. I mentioned I was expanding my business throughout Nashville, which led her to ask me about my business. Ta da! Music to my ears, because I love sharing what I do, and that's how I grow my business.

I shared a one-minute presentation about the company and some product basics. I kept it light and fun, and I ended by asking if she knew a few savvy gals just like her in the Murfreesboro area who she thought might be a great fit for my business. Her attention was piqued, and she wanted to hear more. When we met two days later—at a local coffee shop—I gave her a complete overview of my company and its founders, our products, and of course, the compensation plan. She joined my business a few days later after she had returned home and discussed it with her mom (who also joined my business!). Her mom had given her the green light, and was excited for her business to start.

At a meeting with another business partner who joined my business from another state, I heard her share the story of how she had gotten into the business. She said that our first sit-down meeting was the best two hours she had taken for herself in a really long time. I was moved to tears, having had no idea she felt that way. What's neat is that she had become successful, yet what stuck with her was that initial thrill of taking time for herself and what that meant in terms of her day-to-day life. And it all happened because I shared my gift with a complete stranger. Another great upside to this story is that I now have the cutest chiropractor as a friend and business partner.

About a year ago, I received a call from a woman who lived in Silicon Valley, California. She had been a very successful businesswoman in corporate America, and her husband had also been extremely successful in his work with some of the giant companies of Silicon Valley. Fortunately, she decided that the opportunity with our company was a compelling alternative to jumping back into another corporate gig. After chatting with the couple a few times, they decided to join my team. Both of them work the business full time and within their first 18 months have created a six-figure residual income. They are my company's first "car" recipients from California. Their team is made up of many super-strong, success-driven women, two of whom will also soon be receiving their very own luxury cars!

Speaking of California, I was also in wine country relaxing and enjoying the spa at the Mission Inn. I noticed a nice gentleman doing the same thing and I, of course, shared my business story with him (yes, I have men on my team. It turned out that this gentleman was an ex-NFL football player. The right person is the right person, regardless of chromosomes). He was intrigued and asked me to leave my card at the front desk for him, which I gladly did. After returning home, we had several conversations over the next few months. Once the timing was right for him, he finally joined my team. Today, I have a fabulous group of fun consultants in the wine country, affectionately called, "Team Sonoma." Again, it all happened because I shared my one minute pitch about the opportunity I had been handed. Lucky for me, I now get to go to the wine country every couple of months. We drink wine. We grow our business. Tough job, right? Hey, someone's got to do it. Why not me? Why not you? Glass of wine, anyone?

Let's be clear: Network marketing is not hard work, like manual labor. However, it does take time and a commitment to building your relationships. One of my personal business partners is a nurse anesthetist from Marco Island, FL. She is one of the hardest working women I know. She is a proud mom of two and has a wonderful husband who supports her. She didn't earn that specialized nursing degree by having a microwave mentality. And today, alongside of her medical career, she is building a stellar organization. She put the goal of BFF for her family as her first and foremost goal. I know that within 24 months she will be well on her way to residual income that makes BFF a reality.

Every new relationship enriches your business and your life. When you design your business-building time to fit into your own life, there isn't much sacrifice involved. There are no ticking clocks that dictate your schedule. There are no unappreciative bosses placing unreasonable demands on you. There is no cutthroat attitude to climb faster or higher on some imaginary ladder, or to bump your head against a glass ceiling. The better your team does, the better you do. It truly is the epitome of teamwork.

As with any team, veterans support the rookies. Veterans (sponsors) want their rookies (new team members) to succeed, in part because everyone benefits. Nothing fires up a hungry newbie consultant like getting a check right away. Consultants that produce tend to stick around, and stay in it for the long run. In my company, in the first 48 hours, we launch new consultants' businesses via small gatherings and conference calls that help share the opportunity with their network of friends and colleagues. We immediately start to create a well-rounded business of product consumers and new business partners. Our new consultants see results immediately, which gives them the confidence to build their businesses.

And what's required of me? It's my job to support my new consultants and match their efforts. They get to lean on me and use my expertise to learn and grow. Long-term success always includes being present in your business and attending all local meetings and events, as well as training calls. There are many ways to do this. Since

I began three years ago, I have held a weekly opportunity meeting for my entire organization. We focus on helping new prospects gain the leverage of our team efforts. I also hold weekly trainings to teach my organization how to build big and change their lives by maximizing our company's compensation plan. Daily opportunity calls also offer support to my team and to their prospects as well. As you can see, I talk. Talk at meetings. Talk on the phone. Talk with prospects. Talk with my team. Talk. Talk. Talk. That's what I get paid to do, and I *love* it. I'm a people person. This business rewards one of my inherent gifts as a woman: the gift of gab. I share with everyone, and I am earning a great residual check for doing it. I'm sharing with you now what has worked for me, and it turns out that people who have followed my lead have created significant residual income like mine and enjoy the many benefits of BFF.

I have always attended every event my company offers, from training webinars to the huge conventions they hold across the country for consultants. And now, I am asked to train at our major corporate events! Like me, the people who attend are incredibly more productive post event. I encourage everyone to attend as much as they can. I lead by example. The speed of the leader is the speed of the team. My team builds fast!

Many, if not most, consultants won't stay with you forever. We live in a microwave mentality world. People want instant gratification. If you want instant financial freedom, play the lotto and keep your fingers crossed. But when you're tired of wishing and want to make something happen for yourself, if you want financial freedom in your life, follow my lead to network marketing. It offers you the opportunity to work and get paid for life. This business isn't a cakewalk, but it's worth every second of your initial effort. Once you build it big, it will pay you for the life of the company you joined.

Residual income really is a dream come true, yet it's not as widely understood as you might think. Most people dream about having it all, but not many know

natalia's
action
tip:

Lifestyle Marketing is a path to your success. Share your products and business with everyone, and just be yourself.

that it can be theirs for the taking, and that network marketing is just the vehicle for them to get there. I am living proof of its power. And now I want to help as many women as I can achieve the same level of success that I have. You are already ahead of most of the people out there, as you have kindled your fire and have taken the time to find out what it takes to be financially free. You've gotten started by affirming your intentions and listing people who might join you. Why wait any longer? Build your team. Live your dream.

chapter

your time is now!

*"Success to me is not about money or status or fame,
it's about finding a livelihood that brings me joy and self-
sufficiency and a sense of contributing to the world."*

ANITA RODDICK

Being financially free. It seems like a pretty strong motivator, right? I mean, you can work from home doing what you do best, make unlimited residual income and create both security and opportunity for yourself and your family.

I've talked about several ways of describing our key motivations: hunger, the "why" factor, dreams of the life you want. I've also shared concise and proven ideas for helping you feed that hunger, answer your why, and live that dream life. But I want to make sure you fully understand the importance of motivation to success in network marketing.

Being only mildly hungry, or answering the "why" with "why not?" are probably not strong enough motivators to get you to the dream.

Have you ever noticed that the most satisfying, enjoyable, and meaningful experiences in life are those which have cost something to achieve? I love this quote from Nelson Mandela, who has known the costs of sacrifice perhaps as well as anyone on earth: "There is no easy walk to freedom anywhere, and many of us will have to pass through the valley of the shadow of death again and again before we reach the mountaintop of our desires."

Hard work, sacrifice, and persistence tend to bring about our true successes, whether as individuals, professionals, parents, athletes, significant others, or what have you. I'm reminded of a similar quote from Margaret Thatcher: "I do not know anyone who has gotten to the top without hard work. That is the recipe. It will not always get you to the top, but it will get you pretty near."

Don't get me wrong: I'm not saying you have to be miserable before you're happy, or that you can't be successful without giving up everything to achieve it. Just the opposite, in fact, is true. Happiness is a mindset, and success can be measured as much by what you keep as what you give up.

In network marketing, it's more about persistence than "hard work." You have to be willing to stay with it, to keep moving forward, to be successful. And keeping that momentum is what's behind my asking you about your motivations. If you're not dialed in to the upside of your dream, if it doesn't thrill you to think about achieving it, or make you sad to think about not achieving it, you probably won't stay with it. And that, my friend, would be a tragic mistake. My point is that there will be plenty of failing on the road to BFF, but the only permanent failure can come from not dreaming or taking no action. You need to take a look inside yourself and ask, "What do I really want, why do I want it, how can I get it, and what am I willing to do?"

I'm sticking my neck out to encourage you to be financially free because I know what it's meant for me, and I want the same for you! Success at network marketing is the ultimate self-help program, an earn-while-you-learn education in who you are and what you're capable of that is proof positive that you can do whatever you set your mind to.

One of the best ways to kindle that fire in your belly is to look at what you want, as opposed to what you don't want. I've found that positive motivators are stronger than negative ones. For example, instead of wanting to get out from under the control of a difficult boss, why not think about the power of controlling what you do and when you do it? Instead of wishing you didn't have so many unpaid bills, what about tapping into the excitement of getting your financial house in order so that you're more worried about where to go on vacation than whether you can make your car payment? Independence, security, opportunity, freedom. These should be the basis of your new "wish list."

I once read something that lit a fire in me:

"The wealthiest place on this planet is not the gold mines, diamond mines, oil wells or silver mines of the earth, but the cemetery. Why? Because buried in the graveyard are dreams and visions that were never fulfilled, books that were never written, paintings that were never painted, songs that were never sung, and ideas that died as ideas. What a tragedy, the wealth of the cemetery. I wonder how many thousands, perhaps millions, of people will be poorer because they cannot benefit from the awesome wealth of the treasure of your potential (i.e. legacy): the books you have neglected to write, the songs you have failed to compose, or the inventions you continue to postpone. Perhaps there are millions who need the ministry or the business you have yet to establish. You must maximize your life for the sake of the future. The next generation needs your potential (i.e. legacy)." —Dr. Myles Munroe, Kingdom Success Marketing.

Let's make a quick review of some of the key benefits of BFF through network marketing. If these things would mean the world to you, if you want them so badly it hurts, then you've got the hunger, the "why," and the dream:

✓ **Schedule the life you want.** Create your own timetable and calendar. You control how many hours you work, when you work them, and shift them around your life as needed. Each day is your own.

✓ **Work from home (or wherever you want to be)!** Enjoy the benefits of being your own boss. Make calls in your pajamas. Be there when your kids get home. Manage your household from your household.

✓ **Prioritize your desires.** Children, aging parents, travel, romance, running errands, decorating for the holidays, what do you want to focus on? No longer do you have to get permission to live the life you want.

✓ **Live to work, don't work to live.** Convert your passions and natural skills into success. Feel the fulfillment and satisfaction of following your own drumbeat. This will ignite and motivate you to get up each and every morning excited and energized. Doing what you love is never a chore.

✓ **Develop significant and long-lasting friendships.** Enrich your life with the most amazing girlfriends with whom you can travel, have coffee, lean-on and support, as well as laugh and cry. This is an added benefit of immeasurable value that comes with the business.

✓ **Build self-confidence and self-worth.** These are inherent by-products of this work. Knowing you are financially independent today, tomorrow and for your entire future builds an unshakable foundation for your sense of self.

✓ **Improve your overall health.** Money worries, being overworked and "working for the man" cause stress. Stress makes you sick and tired. Flexibility, doing what you love and solidifying financial freedom provide a much healthier lifestyle physically, emotionally, mentally, and even spiritually.

✓ **Utilize your innate skills as a woman.** Stop trying to make yourself fit into a man's world. Marketing is a natural extension of who we are and how we conduct our lives. We talk! We share! We multi-task! We are flexible! We collaborate! We support each other! These inherently female skills are in complete contrast to those most valued in corporate America. It's only logical and practical for women to work well and succeed when working with other woman.

✓ **Empower your life.** Prepare for the future. Provide for your children the way you desire. Make your time your own. Surround yourself with the comforts and stability of a great home. Own your own life, your own choices and your own joy and satisfaction.

✓ **Create great wealth!** Being Financially Free means peace of mind. Imagine not trying to fall asleep worrying about monthly bills, your family's needs, or your retirement. Relax and sleep soundly! Travel the world. Drive a luxury car (or two!). Carry Louis Vitton luggage. Wear Jimmy Choo shoes. Send your kids to the college of their choice. Support a deserving charity. Whatever your wildest dreams are, you can obtain them. We women can have it all!

natalia's
action
tip:

The expression "Do what you love, the money will follow" is especially true for network marketing. And remember, Success Leaves Clues!

I hope you've taken the time to follow the exercises and respond to the thought questions I've posed throughout this book. I put them there to help you better understand yourself, your motivations and dreams, and whether or not network marketing is a good fit for you. Keep this book with you going forward. You can refer back to it when questions or doubts arise, and you can use it as the foundation for your business going forward. Once you've experienced BFF, the only reason for looking back will be to help others see where you started!

As with most major decisions in life, you'll want to think this through carefully, and do some more research. Check out the resources I've listed. Buy or borrow a couple of the suggested books—and read them! Talk with your partner or closest confidant. Spend some time on the Internet checking out networking opportunities. Find a company that resonates with your passions. And when you do, be ready to jump in with your whole being. Nothing less than financial freedom awaits: You not only deserve it, you owe it to yourself and your family to see what it could mean for you!

One of my favorite songs was written by Rodney Jerkins. It's titled "What are Words?" My favorite line is, "What are words, if you really don't mean them when you say them?" You just finished filling out all these exercises in your own words. Now just go out there and create your dream life!

"Quit hanging on to the handrails . . . Let go. Surrender.
Go for the ride of your life. Do it every day."

MELODY BEATTIE, *Finding Your Way Home*

your
dream team

Use these pages to begin your list of people you'd like to bring onto your team. Remember, start with girlfriends and grow from there.

_____

_____

_____

_____

_____

_____

_____

_____

_____

_____

_____

about
natalia yosco

"The secret of genius is to carry the spirit of the child into old age, which means never losing your enthusiasm."

ALDOUS HUXLEY

Upon meeting Natalia Yosco for the first time, you'll never be the same. Her enthusiasm and joyful spirit leave no question about her astonishingly positive outlook on life. And why not? In just three years Natalia has gone from stay-at-home mom to millionaire mompreneur, and now leads a team of thousands from across the country.

Her *joie de vivre* is not an act: It's part of who she is and what has made her so successful. But she'll be the first to tell you that her success is driven by her team of sharp, dedicated people who share common goals and attitudes, in a company whose founders, values and products fit perfectly with her own values, and those of her team. Natalia's exuberance is also based on what her business gives her: financial freedom, time flexibility, and the icing on the cake—amazing friends!

And Natalia believes in "paying it forward." She always tells those on her team to dream big, and it's her mission to help others enjoy the same financial freedom that she and her family enjoy today. She created this book to help other women experience the joy of working on their own terms, the exhilaration of partnering with sharp, driven people, and the remarkable power and satisfaction of *The New BFF: Being Financially Free.*

To find out more about Natalia and her business, visit **www.NataliaYosco.com** or **www.TheNewBFF.com**

resources

Here's a quick list of my favorite books:

The Compound Effect by Darren Hardy

. . . .

Your First Year in Network Marketing by Mark Yarnell

. . . .

The New Professional: The rise of network marketing as the next great profession by James Robinson

. . . .

Rich Dad, Poor Dad by Robert Kiyosaki

. . . .

The Other 90%: How to unlock your vast untapped potential for leadership and life by Robert K. Cooper

. . . .

Women and Money: Owning the power to control your destiny by Suze Orman

. . . .

The Tipping Point by Malcolm Gladwell

www.TheNewBFF.com